THE FOLLOWING **PARODIES** HAVE BEEN APPROVED FOR
ALL AUDIENCES
BY THE AUTHOR OF THIS BOOK

(BUT MAYBE DON'T SHOW YOUR KIDS PAGES 90 AND 91)

MOVIE TITLE TYPOS

MAKING MOVIES BETTER
BY SUBTRACTING
ONE LETTER

Austin Light

CHRONICLE BOOKS
SAN FRANCISCO

Library of Congress Cataloging-in-Publication Data is available.

ISBN: 978-1-4521-4956-1

Manufactured in China

MIX
Paper from responsible sources
FSC
www.fsc.org
FSC™ C104723

Designed by Neil Egan and Ben Kither
Illustrations by Austin Light

10 9 8 7 6 5 4 3 2 1

Chronicle Books LLC
680 Second Street
San Francisco, CA 94107
www.chroniclebooks.com

Special quantity discounts are available to corporations and other organizations. Contact our premiums department at corporatesales@chroniclebooks.com or at 1-800-759-0190.

Title Key

INTRODUCTION

When I was a kid I would make crappy movies with my brothers and friends. Godzilla movies with toys and paper backgrounds. Over-choreographed living room lightsaber fights that never looked as cool as they felt. Backyard trampoline wrestling extravaganzas with preposterous signature moves. We knew they were crappy when we were making them, but that didn't matter.

We probably spent more time making our movies than we did watching them, which was fine by me—the making was the best part. I eventually stopped making movies, but never stopped making things. I always have to have a project, something fun to work on. Making stuff is in my DNA.

That never-ending desire to make things is what led me to InkTober, a month-long drawing event created by artist Jake Parker that challenges artists to make thirty one ink drawings, one a day. It sounded like fun, but I needed a topic.

Around the same time a coworker showed me a Reddit thread about movie titles with one letter missing. Hilarious what-ifs and could-have-beens, they were movies that would have been fun to make with my brother and friends.

So I did the next best thing. I drew them. Every day I made a new movie with a silly drawing and a new plot description. It was the closest adult me could get to those papercraft Jurassic Parks and ramshackle lightsaber fights of my youth. At the end of the month, a friend helped me post a gallery of the images to share with the Reddit community. And then the Internet exploded.

Suddenly my silly drawings were everywhere. They were viewed more than a million times in less than six hours. Friends of my friends' friends shared them on Facebook. They were featured in a segment on the TV show *@Midnight*. Robert Downey Jr., Molly Ringwald, and Wes Craven all shared them on social media. It was bonkers. It felt like Steven Spielberg found one of my old movies and made it his next blockbuster.

For this book, I've taken my favorites from the initial batch and created even more, all new movies. I've also created new, full-color artwork for all of them (the originals were just quick sketches.) It's been a lot of fun, and I hope you enjoy them as much as I enjoyed making them. And if you find yourself subtracting letters from movie titles (I can't even help it anymore), and you think up a good one, please let me know at www.MovieTitleTypos.com.

0 THINGS
I HATE
ABOUT YOU

Kat realizes there's nothing she
hates about her boyfriend, but
a whole lot she doesn't like.

30

Gerard Butler plays a Spartan warrior who realizes he can't eat and party like he used to if he wants to keep those abs.

ABE

Farmer Hoggett's presidential pig
brings home the blue ribbon at the
County Fair oratory competition.

ALEN

The story of a lonely cashier named
Alen who yearns for something more.
Like eating astronauts.

AW

The mysterious Jigpaw traps a group
of strangers in a house of horrors.
The only way out? Rub his tummy.

BEAUTY
AND THE
BEAT

After a witch turns her best
friend into a dope boom box,
Belle decides to enter *France's
Got Talent*. She crushes it.

TOWMATER CARFACE

CARFACE

A bumbling tow truck accidentally
becomes the new boss of a drug cartel.

CASIO ROYALE

With his cool calculator watch in tow,
super spy James Bond goes undercover
as a high school math teacher to root
out a teenage criminal mastermind.

CAT AWAY

When his owners lock him out
and leave for vacation, Chuck
goes full feral in the back yard.

DAN
OF THE
DEAD

The documentary of how acclaimed method actor Daniel Day Lewis spent a year in a sarcophagus to prepare for his role in *The Mummy 4.*

HEY DANIEL, WE'RE RUNNING OUT FOR COFFEE. YOU NEED ANYTHING IN THERE?

DIRT DANCING

A man pioneers a filthy
new form of dancing,
but can't seem to find a
partner to dance with him.

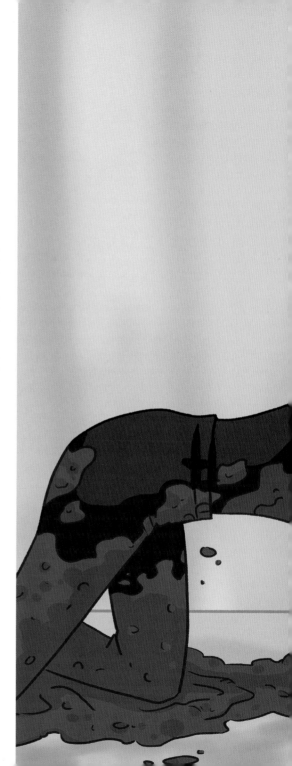

DIVE

Ryan Gosling plays a perplexingly appealing scuba diving guide who gets mixed up in some shady business. He has like twelve lines the whole movie.

FIGHT CUB

When deforestation threatens his
home, one feisty bear fights back. The
one rule of fight cub: DO talk about
fight cub. He's trying to save the forest!

FINDING EMO

An insufferable teenage fish
runs away from home. His father
contemplates searching for him, but
decides to just give him space.

GOOFELLAS

Based on real events, the story
of the rise and fall of East
Jersey Daycare's mob babies.
Directed by Martin Scorsese.

HAPPY FEE

A parking enforcement officer learns
that dancing makes everything
better, even issuing citations.

MOVIE
TITLE TYPOS

HARRY OTTER AND THE PHILOSOPHER'S STONE

A young boy finds out who, and
what, he is. Magic ensues.

HOME
ALOE

When accidentally left behind
by his parents at their vacation
home in Florida, young Kevin
searches the house for a product
to sooth his sizzling sunburn.

INEPTION

Cobb has great ideas, incredible theories, thoughts that could change lives and challenge beliefs. At least, that's what his mom always told him.

I DON'T GET IT.

INGLOURIOUS
BASTERS

In Nazi-occupied France, a group
of guerilla chefs hatch a daring
plan to kill Hitler by feeding him
delicious poison bratwurst.

IT'S A
WONDERFUL
LIE

A boy finds out Santa is totally real,
but also that he's a total jerk.

JURASSIC PAR

Thanks to a loophole in the rules,
two duffer dinos snag a spot on
the PGA tour and golf their way
to the top of the food chain.

MOVIE
TITLE TYPOS

LADY
AND THE
TRAM

The story of a missed connection, and love lost. Lady rides the tram every day, noodle ready, hoping to come across the streetwise Italian delivery boy who charmed her that gloomy September morning.

MOVIE
TITLE TYPOS

MEN

A retired professor helps a
rugged Canadian work through
his aggression as he struggles to
uncover his past. Patrick Stewart
and Hugh Jackman star.

MY BIG
FAT GEEK
WEDDING

A geek girl falls for a non-geek guy. She convinces him—by way of slave Leia lingerie—to participate in the geekiest wedding in the history of weddings.

MOVIE
TITLE TYPOS

OBOCOP

A cyborg police officer moonlights as a sexy jazz artist. The robotic implants might have replaced his heart, but he's still got his soul.

OH BOTHER, WHERE ART THOU?

A convicted felon breaks out of jail with the help of his prison mates and sets off on a cross-state journey to find his missing honey pot.

PETTY WOMAN

When Jessica wears the same
dress as Vivian to the prom, she
makes sure everyone knows it's
very clear who's copying whom.

PIRATE
OF THE
CARIBBEAN

After fleeing his own country on treason charges, a hacker moves his operations to the tropics, hoping to spend his bitcoin treasure in peace.

POLLO 13

After twelve failed
attempts, NASA
finally puts a chicken
on the moon.

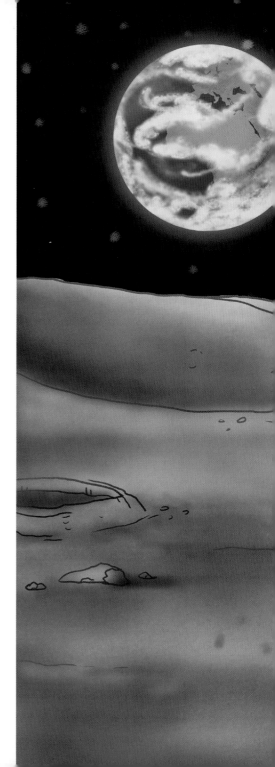

PRETTY
IN INK

Two guys vie for the attention
of an offbeat girl. She tries them
both out, decides to stay single.

PUP
FICTION

When rival dogs come
sniffing around their
territory, two mob
hitmutts start doing "field
neuters." One of them
also explains what dog
food is called in France.

RAINING DAY

On a rainy day in
California, two narcotics
officers skip work to
play board games
and drink cocoa.

RAISIN ARIZONA

The inspiring story of H. I. McDunnough, a poor grape who walked from Phoenix to Hollywood and made it big as a singing raisin.

RAVE

One red-haired Scottish girl. One
dance floor. One unforgettable night.

RON MAN

Heroic small-government advocate
and city employee Ron Swanson
builds a robo suit to keep the town
that he works for from getting any
work done. Also to cook bacon
with the suit's repulsor beam.

SNAKE ON A PLANE

In a world where his peers never leave the ground, one snake dares to take to the skies.

STAR WARS: A NEW HOE

Luke meets an old man in the desert and receives something that used to belong to his father, who as it turns out, was also a moisture farmer.

STAR WARS: THE EMPIRE TRIKES BACK

After crashing his tie fighter on a suburban planet, Darth Vader must get back to the Imperial fleet by any means necessary.

T.:
THE EXTRA-
TERRESTRIAL

A boy meets an aggressive
yet well-meaning, jewelry-
clad alien who pities fools.

TAKE 3

Liam Neeson stars in this *Groundhog Day* inspired movie about an actor cast in a series of nearly identical action movies. How many takes until he's free?

WHERE HAVE YOU TAKEN HER?

THE ARK
KNIGHT

On a massive boat filled with two
of every creature in the world,
one man keeps them all in line.

THE
BREAKFAST
CUB

A young lion learns a valuable
lesson from some unlikely friends
and eats an entire family of gazelles
in a single gruesome morning.
Voiced by Emilio Estevez.

THE EVERENDING STORY

A boy seeking escape from reality
finds a magical book and locks
himself away to read it, only to
find out it never really begins.

THE FAT AND
THE FURIOUS

After a bunch of thugs steal his sweet car, Jerry spirals into a vicious rage-eating depression. He gets super ripped for the next seven sequels.

THE HUGER GAMES

Teenage bodybuilders from the twelve districts go full beast mode as they bulk up for the annual Huger Games.

THE LORD
OF THE RIGS

The story of one man's
unhealthy obsession
with his truck.

THE PRINCESS
AND
THE FRO

A waitress goes natural and
rocks a fro. Later she becomes
a princess for some reason.

IT'S CONCEIVABLE

THE
PRINCESS
RIDE

After years apart, two lovers are
reunited only to discover neither
loves what the other has become.

MOVIE
TITLE TYPOS

THE
SILENCE OF
THE LABS

An in-depth documentary
profile of Doctor Hannibal
Lecter, inventor of the
anti-bark collar.

TWILIGHT: NEW MOO

A young man competes with a
rival suitor as he tries to win a
moody girl's heart with his hot
bovine transformation skill.

VAN
ALMIGHTY

One man, blessed with
gifts from God, creates
the most metal van
in all of metaldom.
And it was good.

WAR OF
THE
WORDS

Tom Cruise stars in the most
intense spelling bee ever imagined.
Explosions! Sweaty brows!
Eastern European etymology!

ACKNOWLEDGMENTS

This book wouldn't have happened without several people. My lovely wife Brooke, thank you for your unwavering support, and for putting up with me doodling at the dinner table. The Reddit community, thank you for the incredible response. Ed Mendoza, thanks for showing me the original typos thread, I owe you one. Taylor Goddard, thank you for posting my original sketches, and your endless enthusiasm. My editor Steve Mockus, thanks for helping me turn my silly doodles and gags into something special. Chronicle designer Neil Egan, thank you for making the book look fantastic. Sarah Marino and my Oatley Academy classmates, thanks for your advice, and boosting my confidence in the process. And finally, thanks to everyone who liked my art, emailed me movie suggestions, and shared in the fun while my goofy drawings exploded the Internet. That was fun.

ABOUT THE AUTHOR

Austin Light is a writer, illustrator, and mega geek who lives and works in Charlotte, North Carolina. This is his first book. See more of his work at www.austindlight.com and www.MovieTitleTypos.com